THE LIZARD LIBRARY™

The Green Iguana

Jake Miller

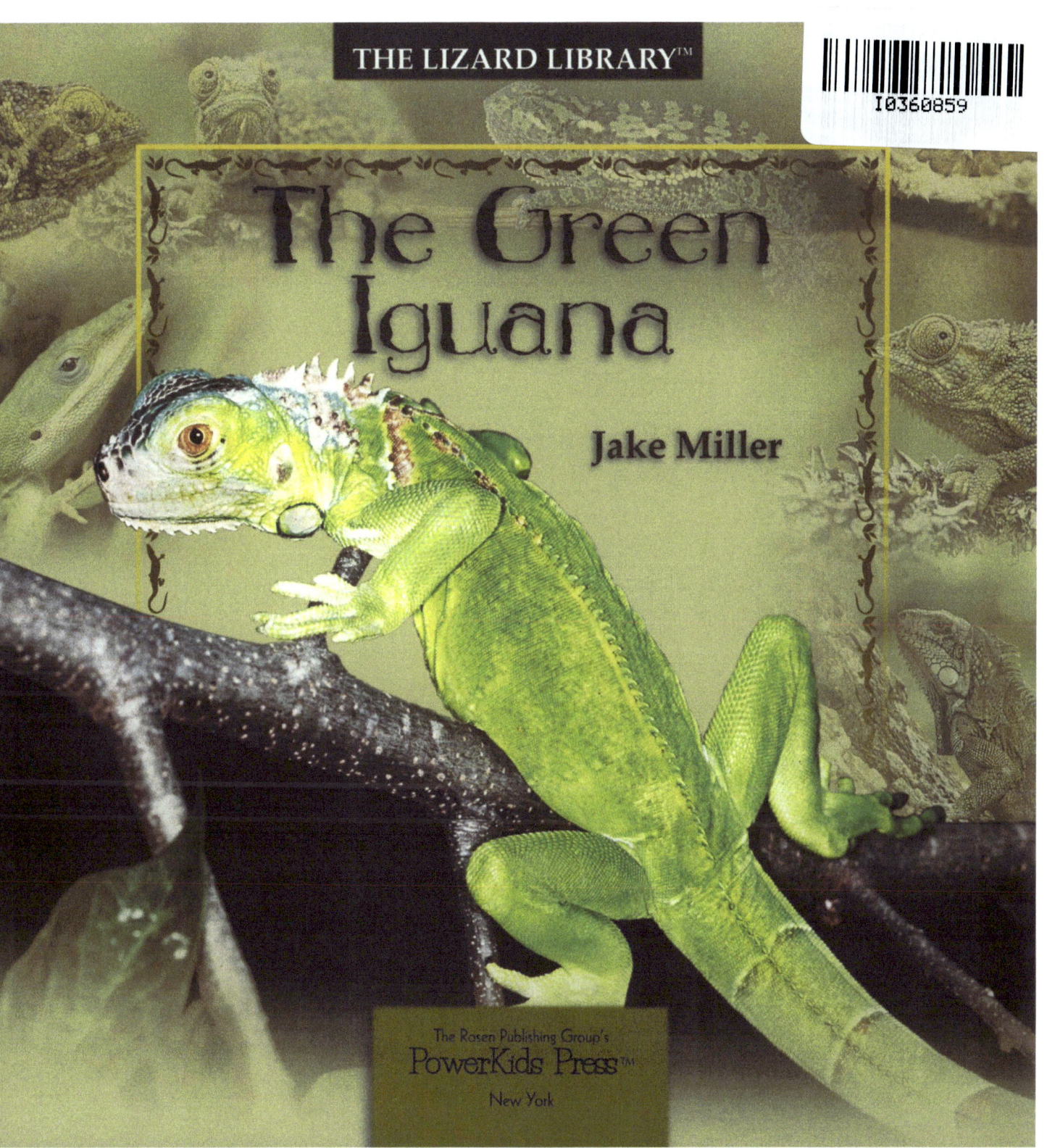

The Rosen Publishing Group's
PowerKids Press™
New York

Published in 2003 by The Rosen Publishing Group, Inc.
29 East 21st Street, New York, NY 10010

Copyright © 2003 by The Rosen Publishing Group, Inc.

All rights reserved. No part of this book may be reproduced in any form without permission in writing from the publisher, except by a reviewer.

First Edition

Editor: Nancy MacDonell Smith
Book Design: Maria E. Melendez
Book Layout: Colin Dizengoff

Photo Credits: Cover and title page © Paul Freed/Animals, Animals; pp. 4, 10, 11, 16 © Zig Leszczynski/Animals, Animals; pp. 5, 15 © E. R. Degginger/Animals Animals; p. 6 © Roland Seitre/Peter Arnold, Inc.; p. 7 © Ken Cole/Animals, Animals; pp. 8, 19 © Fred Bruemmer/Peter Arnold, Inc.; p. 9 © Mella Panzella/Animals Animals; p. 12 © Fritz Prenzel/Animals, Animals; p. 13 © Peter Arnold, Inc.; p. 20 (bear) © Digital Stock; pp. 20 (iguana), 22, page border images © Digital Vision.

Miller, Jake, 1969–
The green iguana / Jake Miller.— 1st ed.
    p. cm. — (The Lizard library)
Includes bibliographical references (p.   ).
Summary: Describes the life cycle and habits of the green iguana.
  ISBN 13: 978-1-4358-3695-2
1. Green iguana—Juvenile literature. [1. Green iguana.] I. Title.
  QL666.L25 M56 2003
  597.95'42—dc21

                                                                                        2001007781

Manufactured in the United States of America

Contents

1. The Giant Green Iguana — 5
2. Land of the Iguana — 6
3. Keeping Warm, Keeping Cool — 9
4. Eat Your Vegetables — 10
5. Home Sweet Home — 13
6. Iguana Parents — 14
7. Iguana Babies — 17
8. Watching (and Tasting) the World Around Them — 18
9. Self-Defense for Iguanas — 21
10. Iguanas as Pets — 22
    Glossary — 23
    Index — 24
    Web Sites — 24

A full-grown green iguana is usually about 3 feet (1 m) long, although some get even bigger.

The Giant Green Iguana

You probably will not be surprised to learn that the green iguana is green. If you know that some people also call the green iguana the giant green iguana, you also won't be surprised to learn that they are very big. Some green iguanas can grow to be more than 6 ½ feet (2 m) long from tip to tail! Iguanas have very long tails. Their tails make up about half of their body length. Green iguanas have floppy **spikes**, which look like the teeth of a comb, on their necks and backs. Green iguanas have stocky bodies and four long, strong legs. Each of their four feet has five toes, and each toe has a sharp claw.

Green iguanas are good climbers.

Land of the Iguana

Green iguanas live in North America, Central America, and South America. They are native to Central America and South America, including such countries as Mexico, Brazil, and Paraguay. They are also native to some islands in the Caribbean Sea. Wild iguanas also now live in some parts of Florida and Texas in the United States. These American iguanas used to be pets. They either escaped or were let go by pet owners who couldn't take care of them when they got too big. Green iguanas' favorite places to live are forests that grow around rivers, because they like to swim and climb.

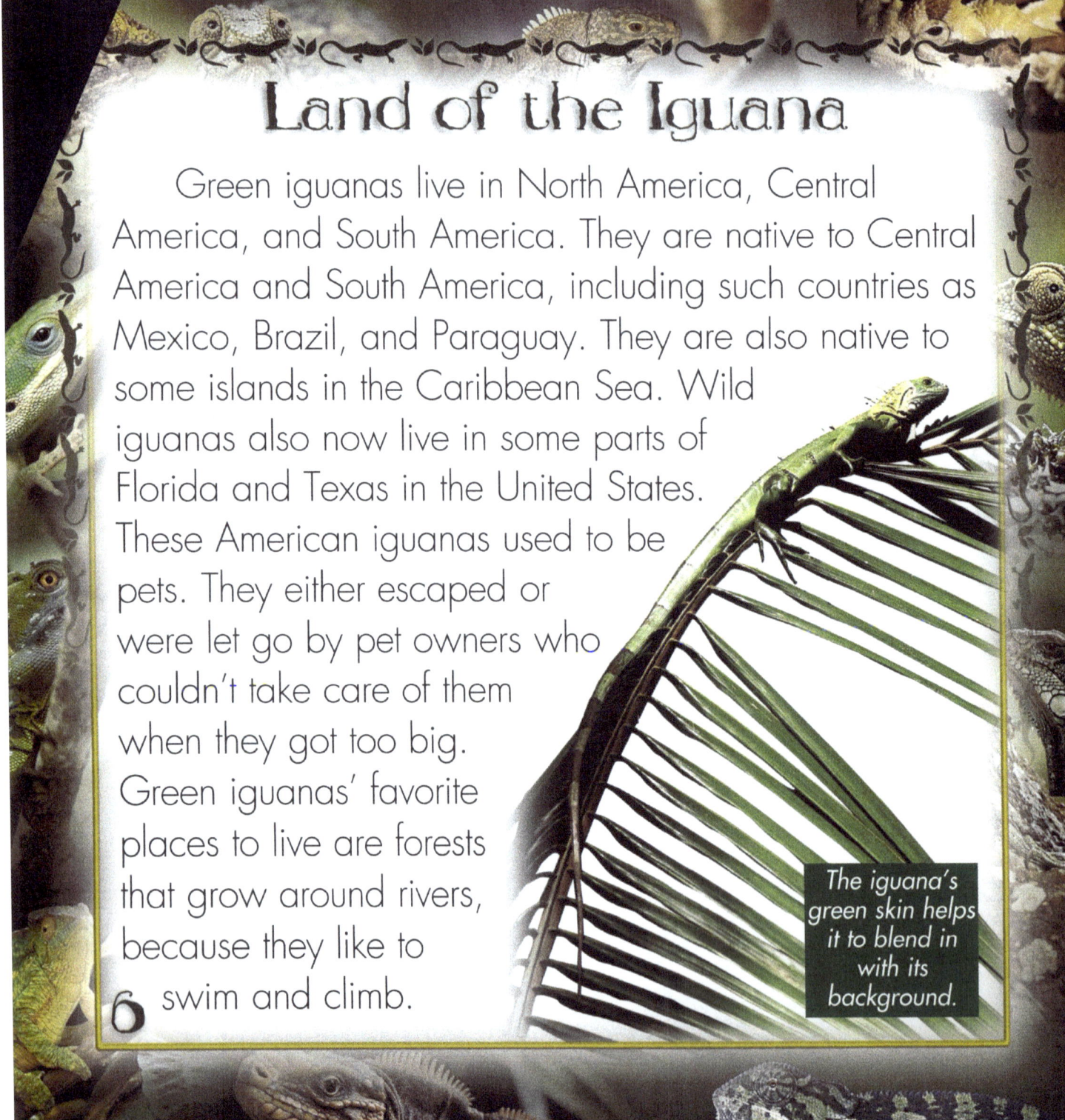

The iguana's green skin helps it to blend in with its background.

Green iguanas are very tough. They can fall from 40 to 50 feet (12–15 m) high to the ground without getting hurt.

When a male iguana spreads its dewlap, the dewlap looks like a frilly umbrella. The rest of the time the dewlap hangs loosely from the iguana's neck.

Keeping Warm, Keeping Cool

Green iguanas sleep in the branches of trees. When these iguanas wake up in the morning, the first thing they do is sit in the sun. Iguanas are **cold-blooded**. They like to sit where it is between 95°F and 98°F (35°–37°C). They sit in the sun until their body **temperature** is between 80°F and 90°F (27°–32°C). If it gets too hot where they are sitting, iguanas move to a cooler place. Male iguanas have big flaps of skin on their necks called **dewlaps**. They can use their dewlaps to help control their body temperature. When an iguana stretches out its dewlap in the sun, its whole body warms up faster.

Green iguanas are active during the day. They sleep at night.

Eat Your Vegetables

Each day green iguanas spend a total of about 45 minutes eating in either the morning or the afternoon. They spend the rest of their time resting. Green iguanas are usually **herbivores**. Sometimes young iguanas will catch and eat insects. However, green iguanas usually eat vegetables, leaves, flowers, and fruits from many different kinds of plants. Iguanas have many small, even-sized teeth to help them eat. They use their teeth to grab hold of a leaf or a piece of fruit and then rip it off the vine or the tree branch. Unlike humans, iguanas grow new teeth all the time to replace old ones when they break or get worn down. Most adult humans have only 32 teeth. A green iguana may have anywhere from 80 to 120 teeth!

Green iguanas don't chew their food. Instead they swallow things, such as this cricket, whole.

Green iguanas like to eat young, fresh leaves rather than old, tough leaves. They like fruit when it is perfectly ripe.

Green iguanas don't like to share their space with other animals, not even other iguanas.

Home Sweet Home

Green iguanas are **solitary** animals. They will mark the places where they live with their **scent** to make sure no other iguanas come into their **territory**. Wherever they walk, iguanas leave behind trails of their scent. Male iguanas are especially protective of their territory. If two males either smell or see each other, each will try to scare the other one away. The male iguanas stick out their dewlaps, stand sideways, and try to look as big as possible. They do push-ups and bob their heads up and down. If neither one backs down, they may fight. Usually neither one gets hurt. The fight is like a wrestling match to see who is the strongest. The weak iguana gives up and goes away.

Green iguanas leave their scent on leaves.

Iguana Parents

Green iguanas **mate** at about the same time every year. The exact time depends on conditions such as temperature and rainfall. Male iguanas fight one another to see who gets to be a father. Only the strongest males get to mate. Once a female is ready to lay her eggs, she digs a nest that is from 3 to 6 feet (1–2 m) long and 2 feet (.5 m) deep. The mother lays her eggs in the bottom of the nest, then covers the nest with sand and goes away. Iguana parents don't take care of their young after the eggs are laid. Green iguanas can lay between 10 and 70 eggs at a time. The average number of eggs laid at one time is between 35 and 45. The eggs are white, leathery ovals of about 1 ½ inches by 1 inch (38 x 25 mm). Each egg weighs between 0.3 and 0.4 ounces (8.5–12 g). Some animals, such as humans, have a few large babies that are all more likely to live long lives. Iguanas have many small babies, but only between 3 and 10 of the babies from a nest reach adulthood. Some are eaten by other animals. Some can't find enough food. Some die from disease.

In parts of Central America and South America, people eat green iguana eggs. People say the eggs taste like cheese.

Young iguanas are bright green. Their color gets duller as they get older.

Green iguanas grow quickly. By the time they are a year old, they may be 3 feet (1 m) long. By the time they are 4 years old, they may be 6 feet (2 m) long.

Iguana Babies

Depending on the temperature, it takes between 90 and 120 days for the eggs to hatch. The newborn lizards, known as **hatchlings**, are from 7 to 10 inches (18–25 cm) long. Sometimes the eggs hatch during the day, and sometimes they hatch at night. If they hatch at night, it takes longer for the hatchlings to warm up and become active, but they are safer because their enemies can't see them. If they hatch during the day, they become active more quickly, but they are easy targets for hawks and other **predators**. Iguanas that hatch during the day stay in groups until they get far enough away from the nest to be safe from waiting predators. In a group, iguanas are safer than they would be if they were alone. Iguanas that hatch at night don't need to stay in groups, and each makes its way alone. When they are from 1 ½ to 3 years old and from 28 to 40 inches (71–102 cm) long, they are **mature** and are ready to be parents.

Watching (and Tasting) the World Around Them

Green iguanas have excellent eyesight. They spend a lot of their time just sitting in trees, watching the world around them. Besides their two main eyes, iguanas also have a third eye on the top of their heads. This eye looks straight up. The third eye can't see very well, but it can **detect** differences between light and dark, so an iguana can sense when something is moving above it. Many of the animals that **prey** on iguanas in the wild, such as hawks and humans, attack from above. This can make it hard to pick up a pet iguana because the lizard will think it is in danger.

Iguanas can also smell what is happening around them. They sense smells more with their mouths than

Green iguanas stick out their tongues when they want to smell the world around them.

with their noses. Inside their mouths they have a special **sensory organ** called **Jacobson's organ**, which helps them to detect all kinds of smells. With this organ, they can smell predators, food, and other iguanas.

Self-Defense for Iguanas

Green iguanas have many natural enemies. Snakes, turtles, fish, birds, otters, bears, and jaguars all like to eat iguanas. Some people like to eat iguanas, too. People also capture iguanas to sell as pets. When an iguana is in danger, it likes to take the easy way out. If it is on a branch that hangs over a stream, it will jump off the branch and swim away from trouble instead of trying to fight. Iguanas use their tails to help them balance when they climb trees and to help them swim swiftly through the water. If there is no way to escape and iguanas need to fight to protect themselves, they can also use their tails as weapons by snapping them like whips. If a predator catches an iguana's tail, the tail will fall off and a new one will grow in its place.

Green iguanas use their sharp claws and teeth to protect themselves from their enemies.

Iguanas as Pets

Green iguanas have special **requirements** that can make them difficult to keep as pets. Full-grown iguanas need cages the size of bedrooms. They have to eat special foods to stay healthy. Their room should be between 82°F and 95°F (28–35°C) during the day and between 65°F and 72°F (18–22°C) at night. Still, many lizard lovers keep iguanas as pets. With care, iguanas can be tamed. However, they still need to be treated carefully. Even a tame iguana can bite or scratch its owner.

Many people don't realize that a 10-inch (25-cm) baby iguana will grow up to be a 6-foot (2-m) adult.

Glossary

cold-blooded (KOHLD-bluh-did) Having a body temperature that changes with the surrounding temperature.
detect (dih-TEKT) To find out or discover.
dewlaps (DOO-laps) Folds of skin under an animal's neck.
hatchlings (HACH-lings) Baby animals that have just come out of their eggs.
herbivores (ER-bih-vorz) Animals that eat plants.
Jacobson's organ (JAY-cub-sunz OR-gun) A kind of sensory organ that helps lizards' sense of smell.
mate (MAYT) When a male and female join together to make babies.
mature (muh-TOOR) Full grown.
predators (PREH-duh-terz) Animals that kill other animals for food.
prey (PRAY) To hunt for food.
requirements (rih-KWYR-mints) Things that are needed.
scent (SENT) A smell.
sensory organ (SENS-ree OR-gun) An organ such as an eye or a taste bud that provides the brain with information about the world.
solitary (SAH-lih-tehr-ee) Liking to be alone.
spikes (SPYKS) Sharp, pointy things shaped like a spear or a needle.
temperature (TEM-pruh-cher) How hot or cold something is.
territory (TEHR-uh-tor-ee) Land or space that is protected by an animal for its use.

Index

B
babies, 15
Brazil, 6

C
Central America, 6
cold-blooded, 9

D
dewlaps, 9, 13

E
eggs, 14, 17
eyes, 18

F
Florida, 6

H
hatchlings, 17
herbivores, 10

J
Jacobson's organ, 19

M
mate, 14

N
North America, 6

P
predator(s), 17, 19, 21
prey, 18

S
scent, 13
smell(s), 18–19
South America, 6

T
tail(s), 5, 21
teeth, 10
temperature, 9, 14, 17
territory, 13
Texas, 6
trees, 9, 21

Web Sites

Due to the changing nature of Internet links, PowerKids Press has developed an online list of Web sites related to the subject of this book. This site is updated regularly. Please use this link to access the list:

www.powerkidslinks.com/ll/griguan/

www.ingramcontent.com/pod-product-compliance
Lightning Source LLC
Chambersburg PA
CBHW041121070526
44584CB00002B/240